27 SOUTH FULTON

Guess What?
**Text and Graphics
By Beau Gardner
Lothrop, Lee & Shepard Books
New York**

Horse

Introduction

This is a book that invites you to "guess what" animal is being presented. First, it shows you a small portion of the entire animal in bright, playful colors. The correct answer then appears in gray on the back of each color page.

Beau Gardner

With special thanks to Shelley Creech for all of her creative contributions

Copyright © 1985 by Beau Gardner
All rights reserved. No part of this book may be reproduced or utilized in any form or by any means, electronic or mechanical, including photocopying, recording or by any information storage and retrieval system, without permission in writing from the Publisher. Inquiries should be addressed to Lothrop, Lee & Shepard Books, a division of William Morrow & Company, Inc., 105 Madison Avenue, New York, New York 10016.
Printed in the United States of America.
First Edition
1 2 3 4 5 6 7 8 9 10

Library of Congress Cataloging and Publication Data
Gardner, Beau.
Guess What?

Summary: The reader examines a boxed illustration of part of an animal's body and tries to guess the identity of the animal, which is revealed by the complete illustration on the next page.
1. Animals—Pictorial works—Juvenile literature.
2. Picture puzzles—Pictorial works—Juvenile literature.
[1. Animals—Pictorial works. 2. Picture puzzles]
I. Title.
QL49.G247   1985   596'.0022'2   85-242
ISBN 0-688-04982-6
ISBN 0-688-04983-4 (lib. bdg.)

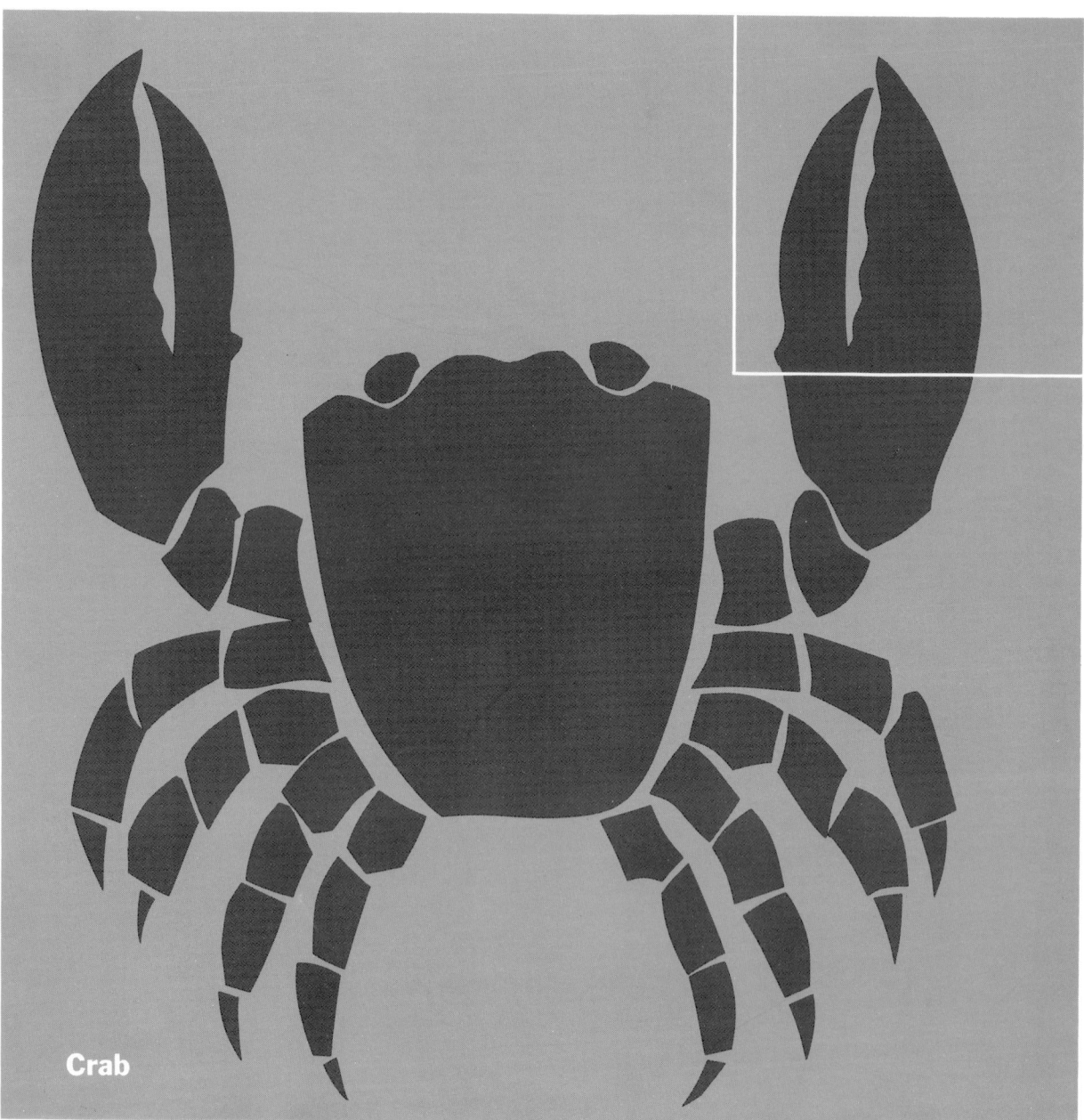

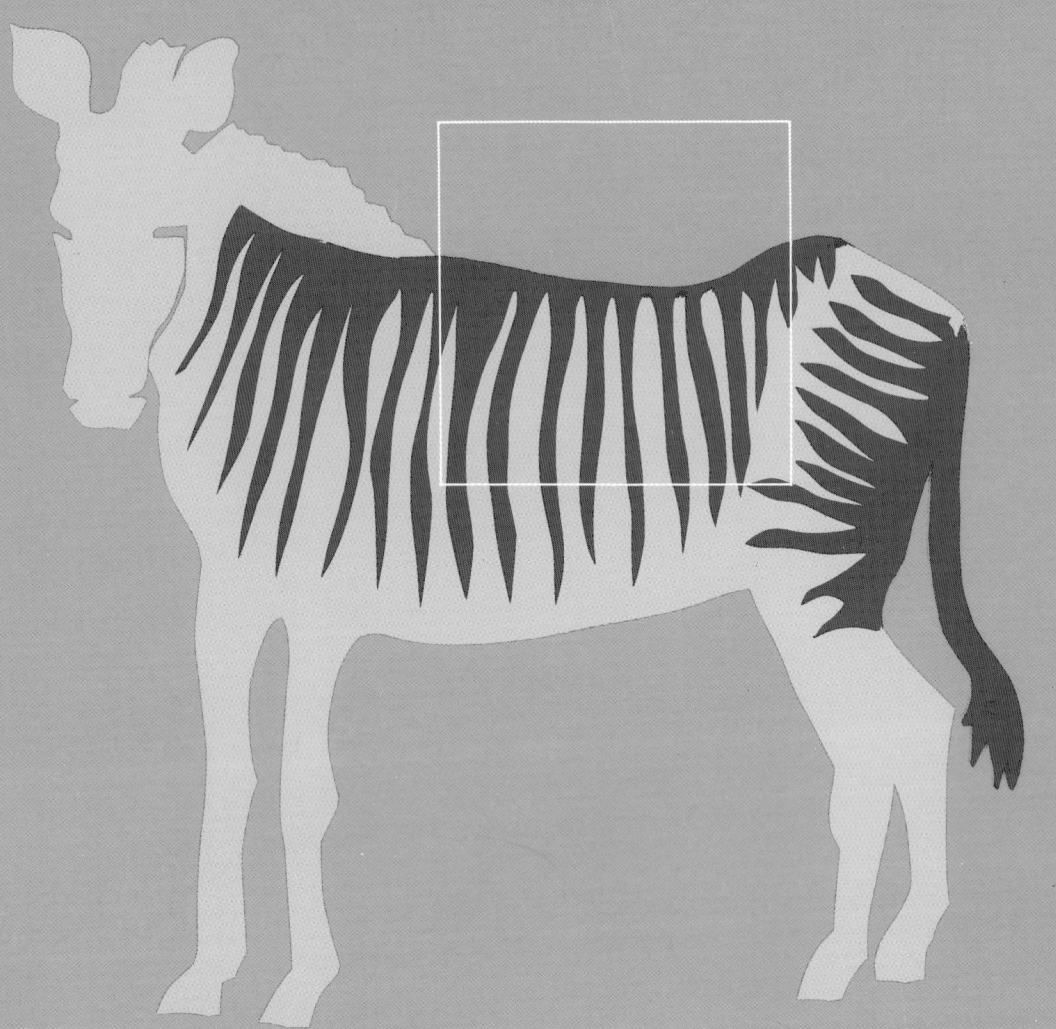

Snail

Dolphin

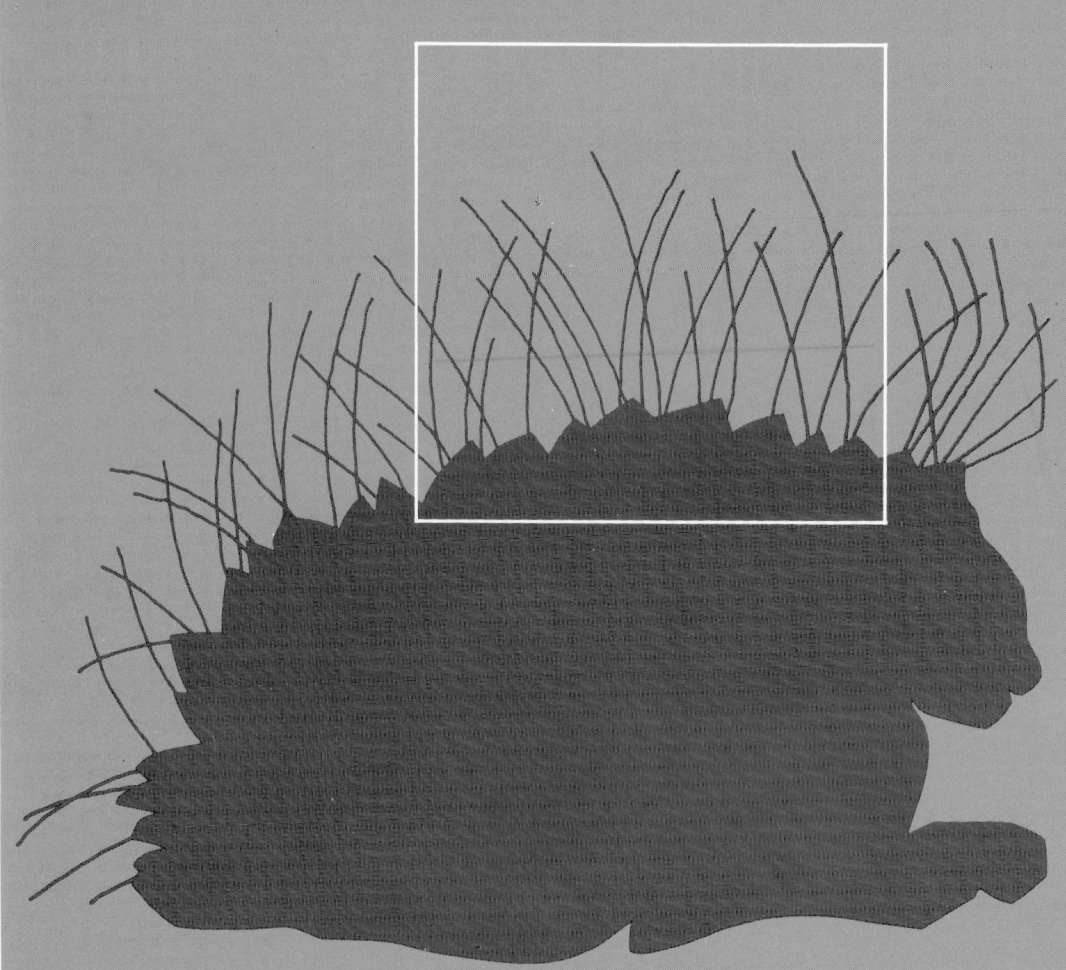

Porcupine

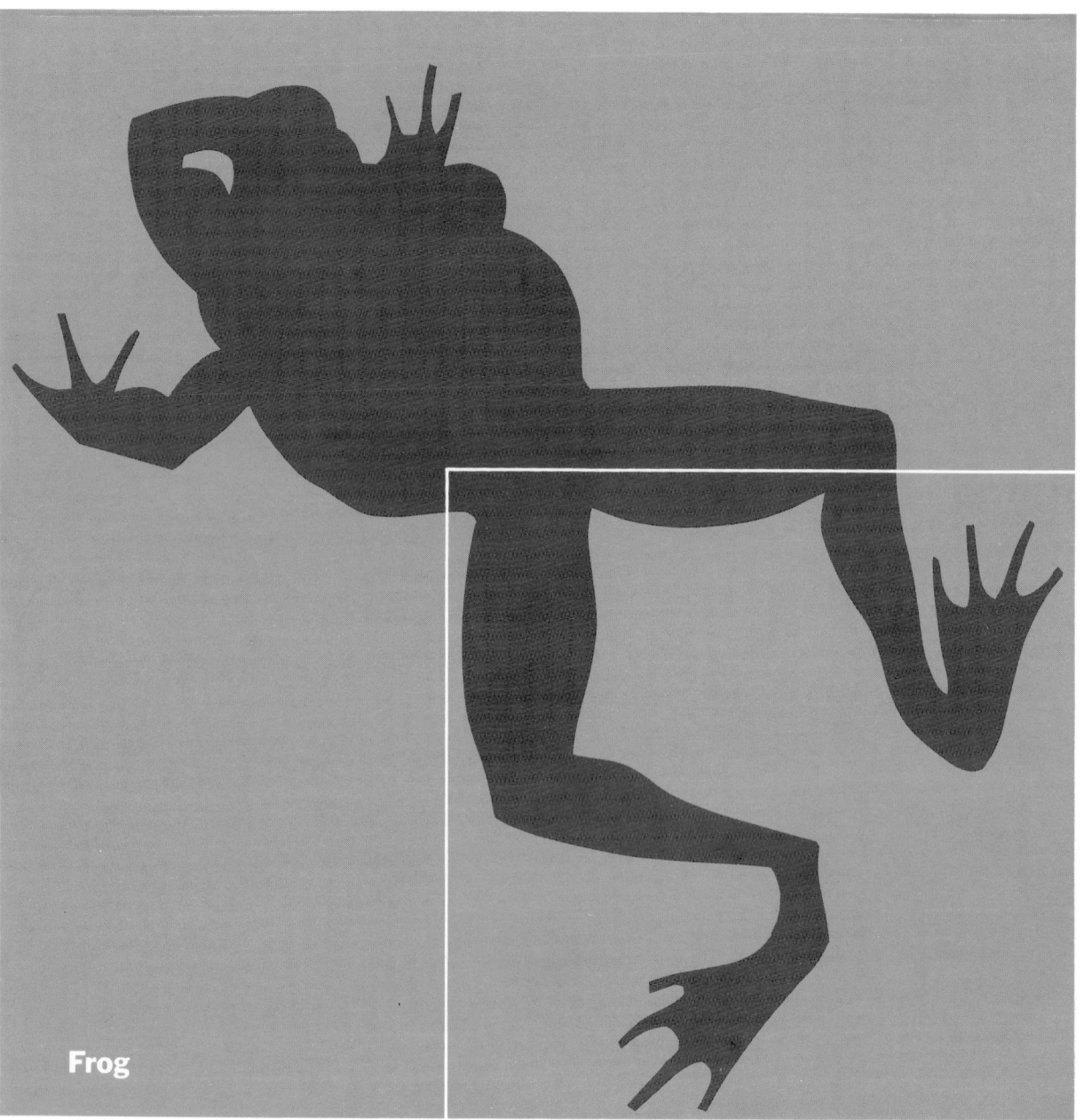

Snake

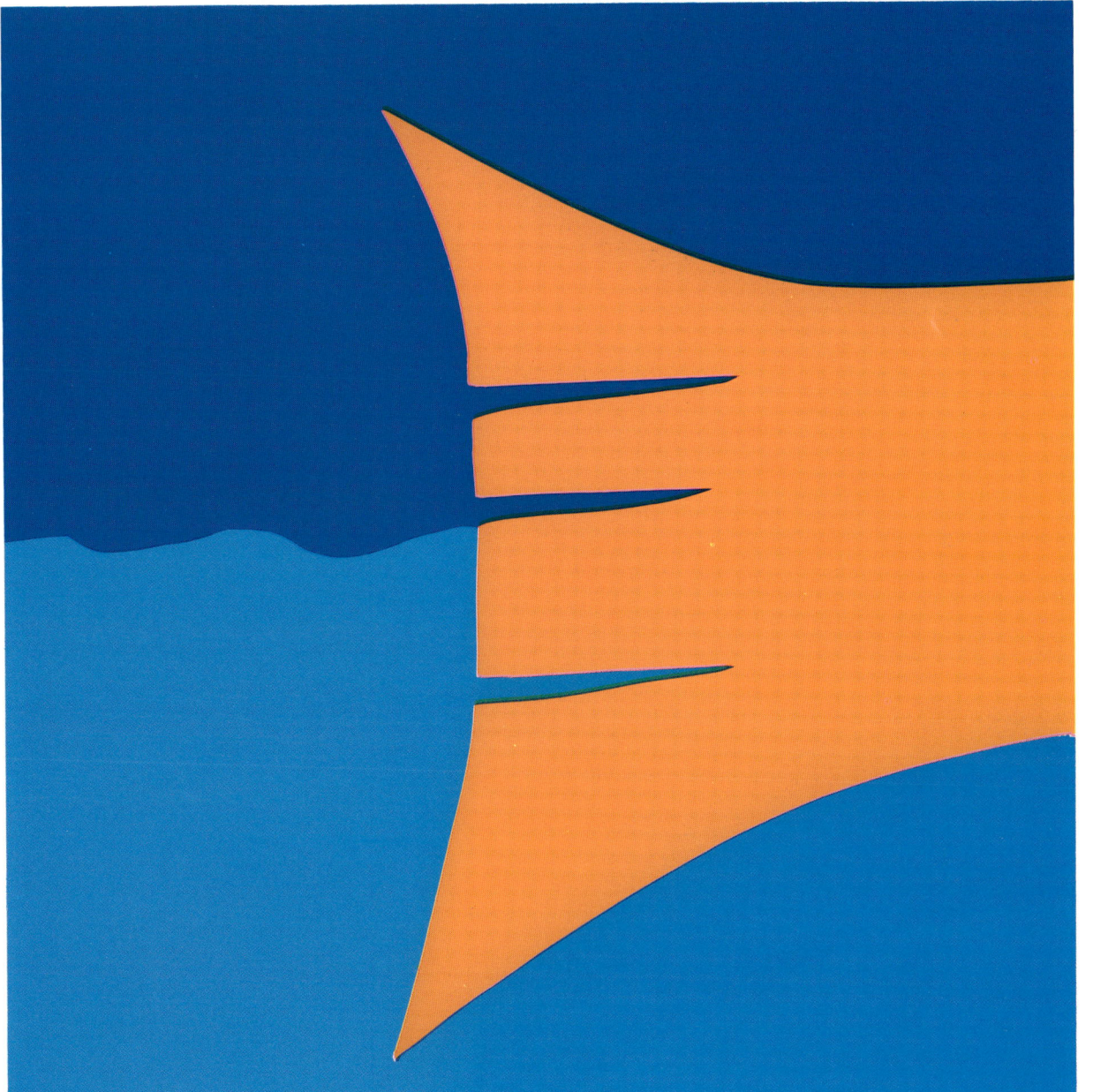

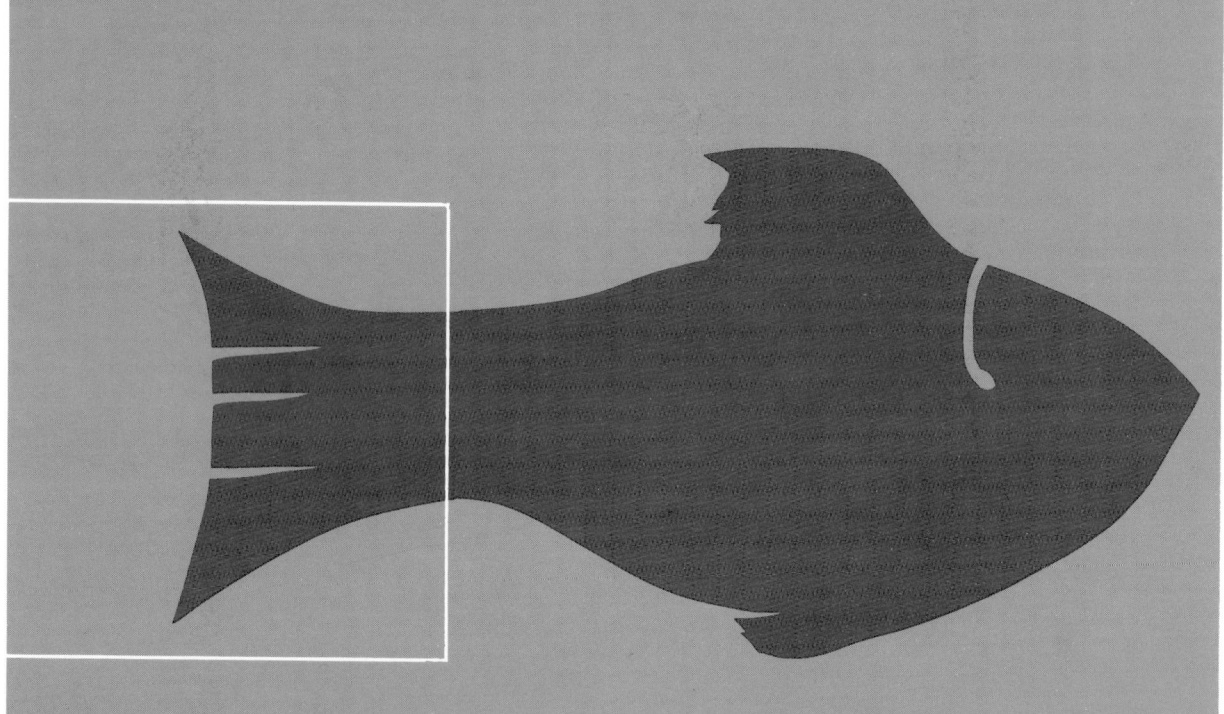

Bat

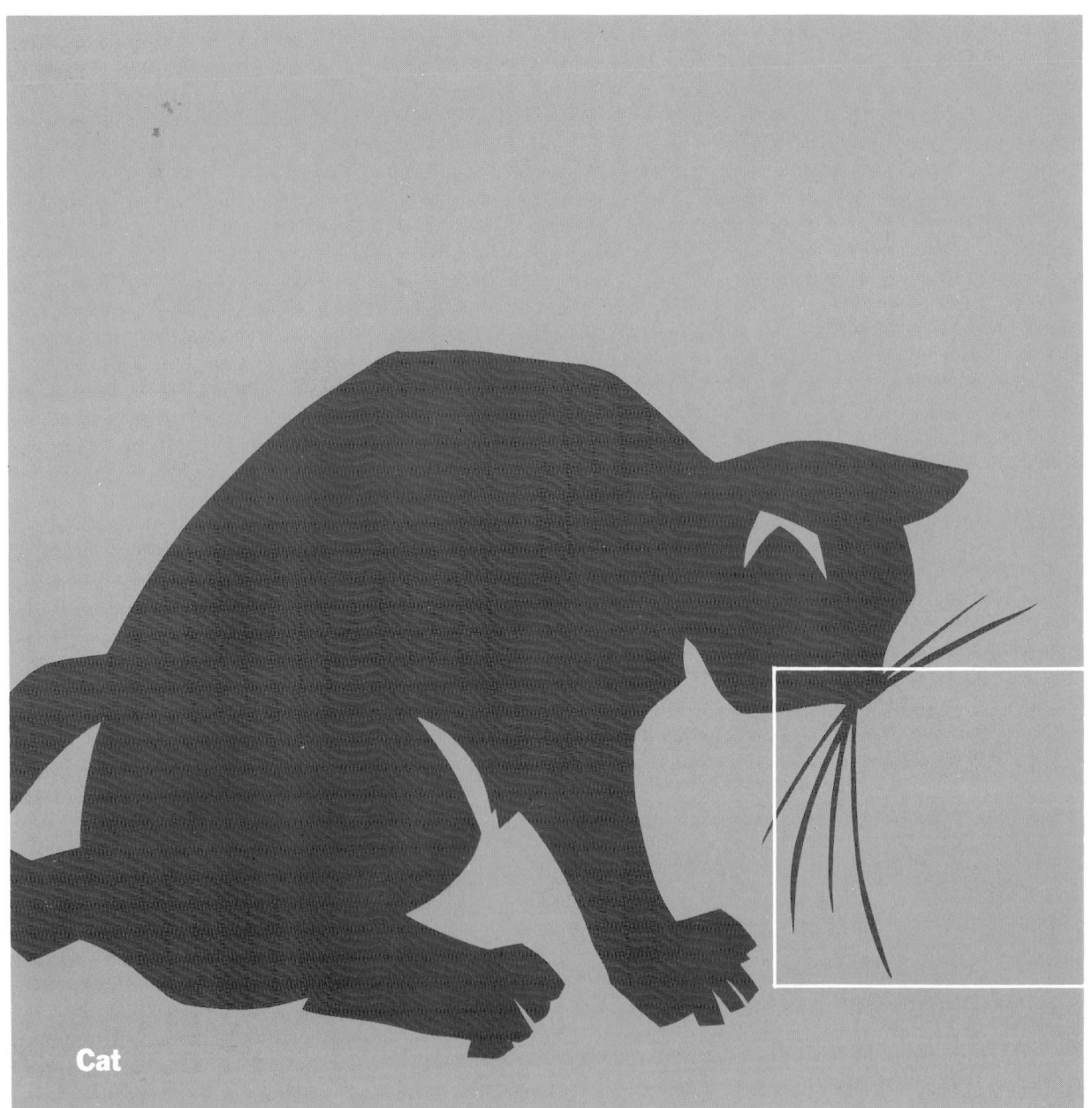

Anteater

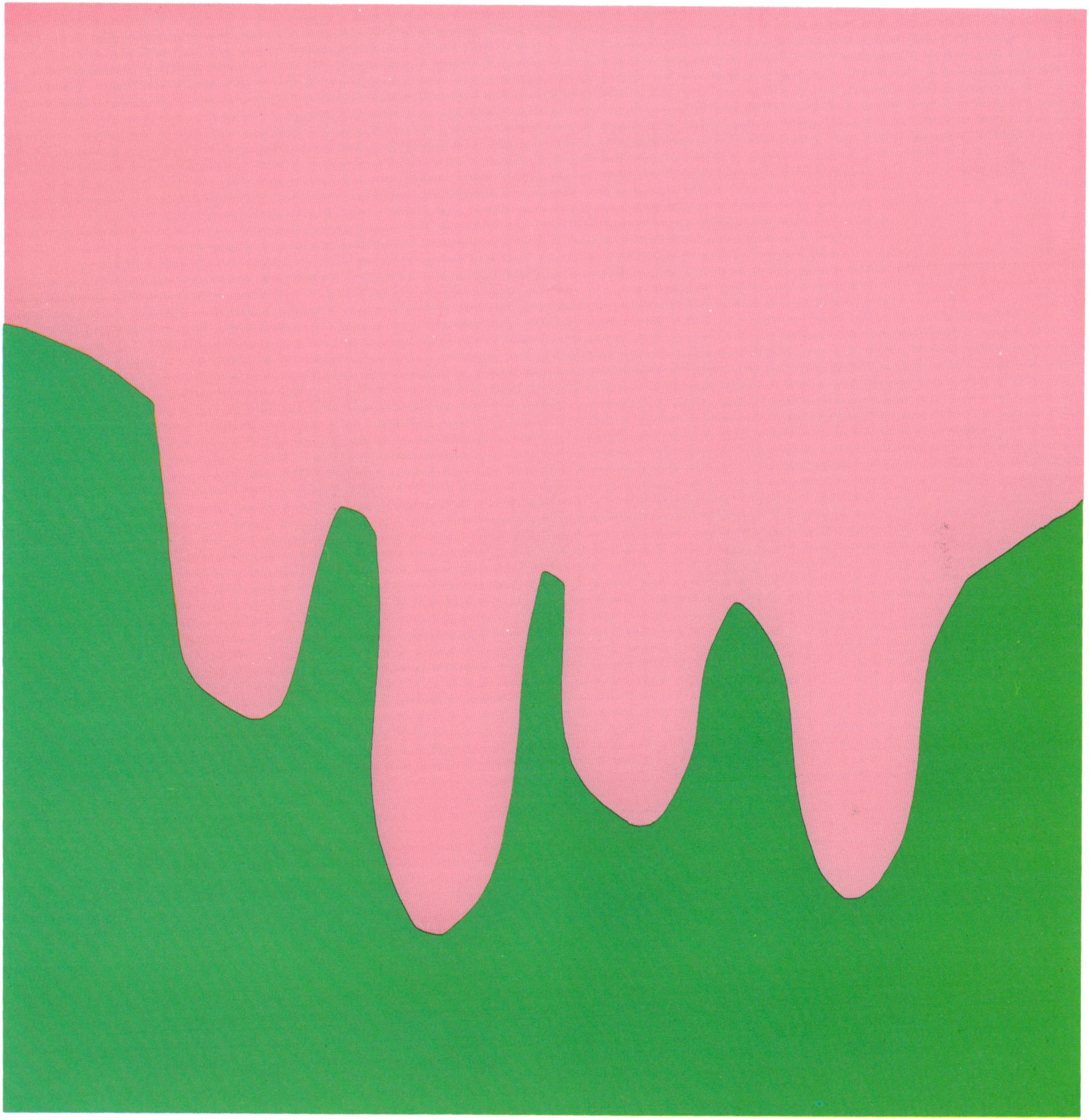

Cow

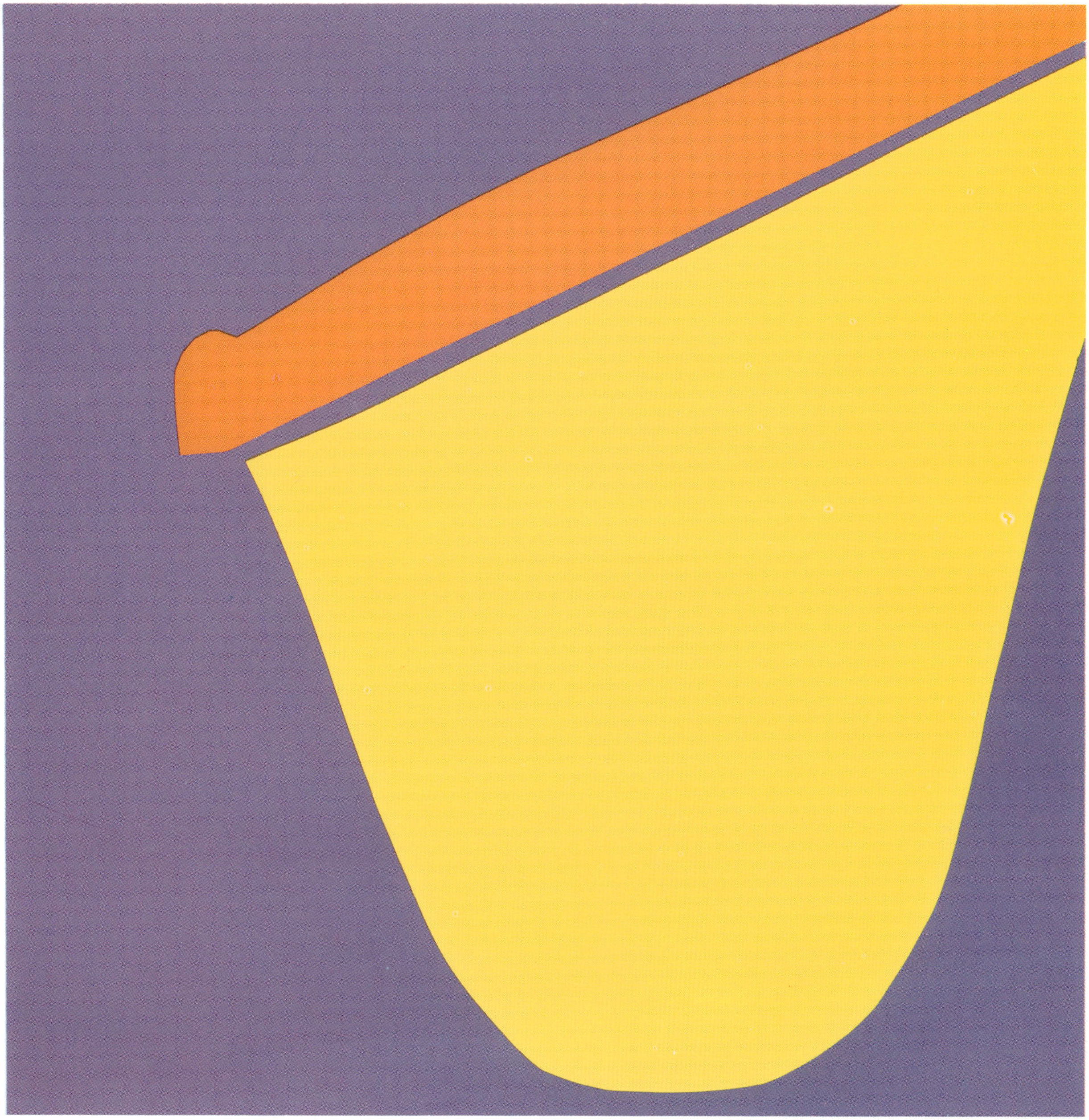

Pelican

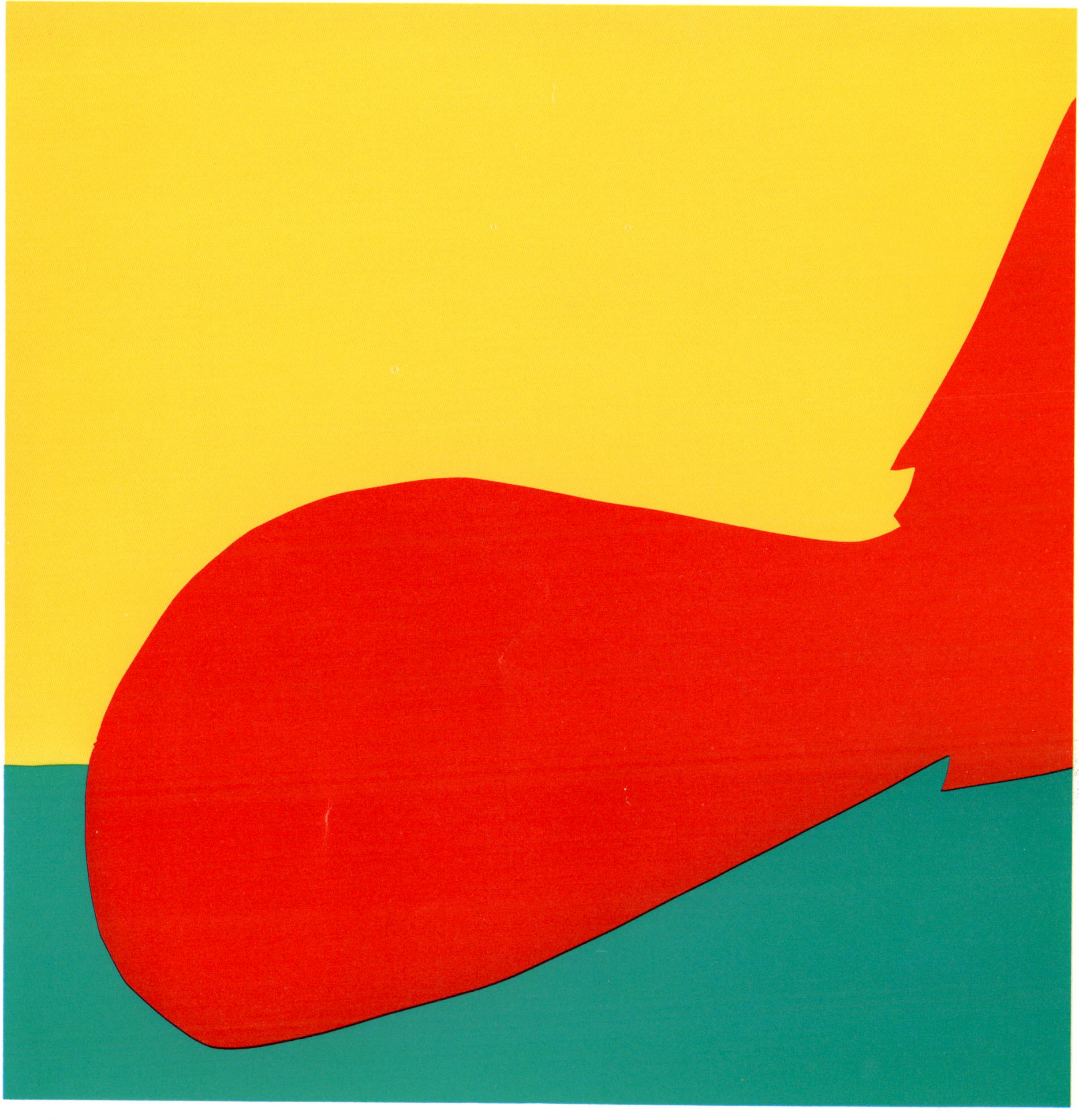

Beaver

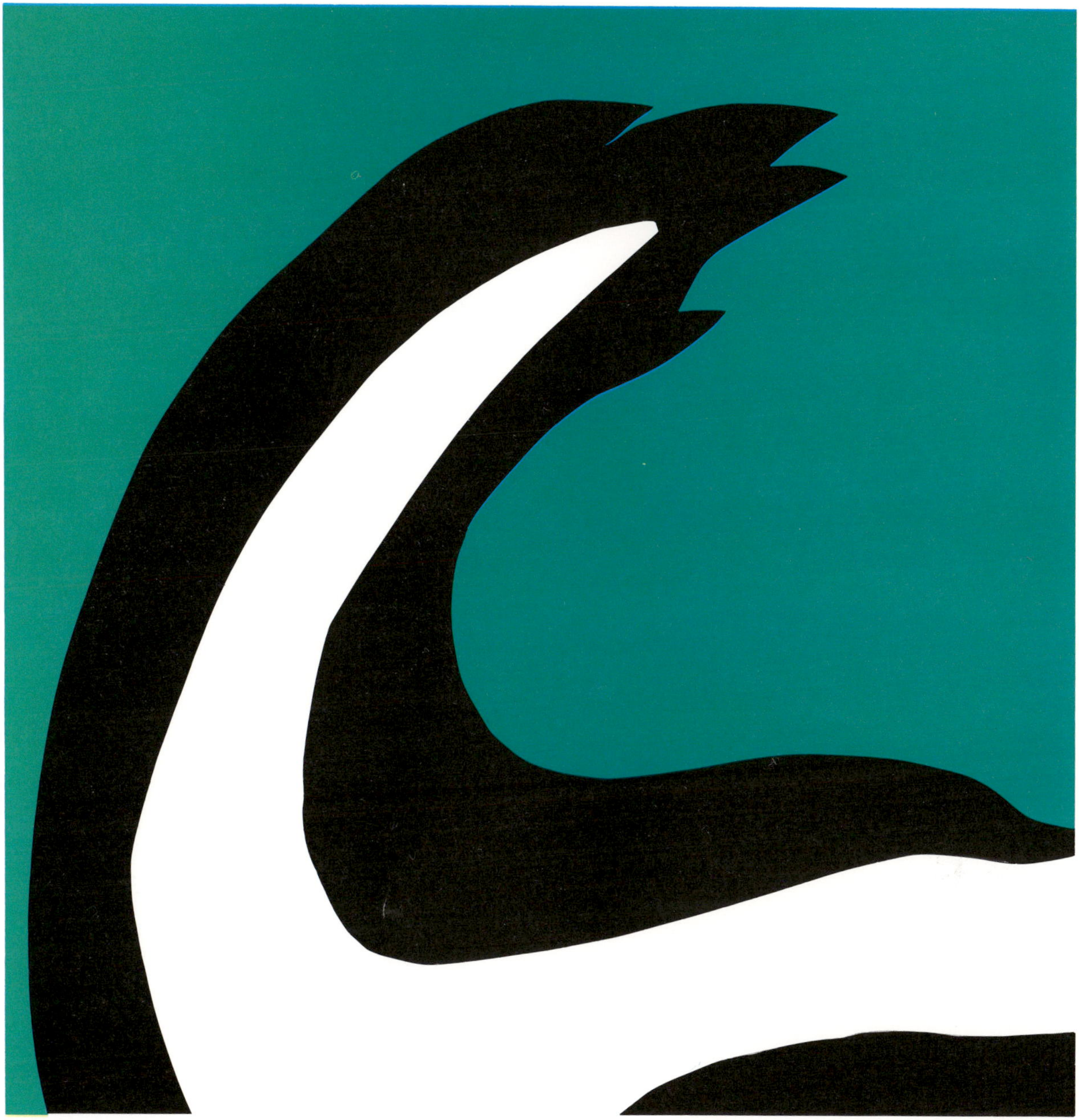

Skunk

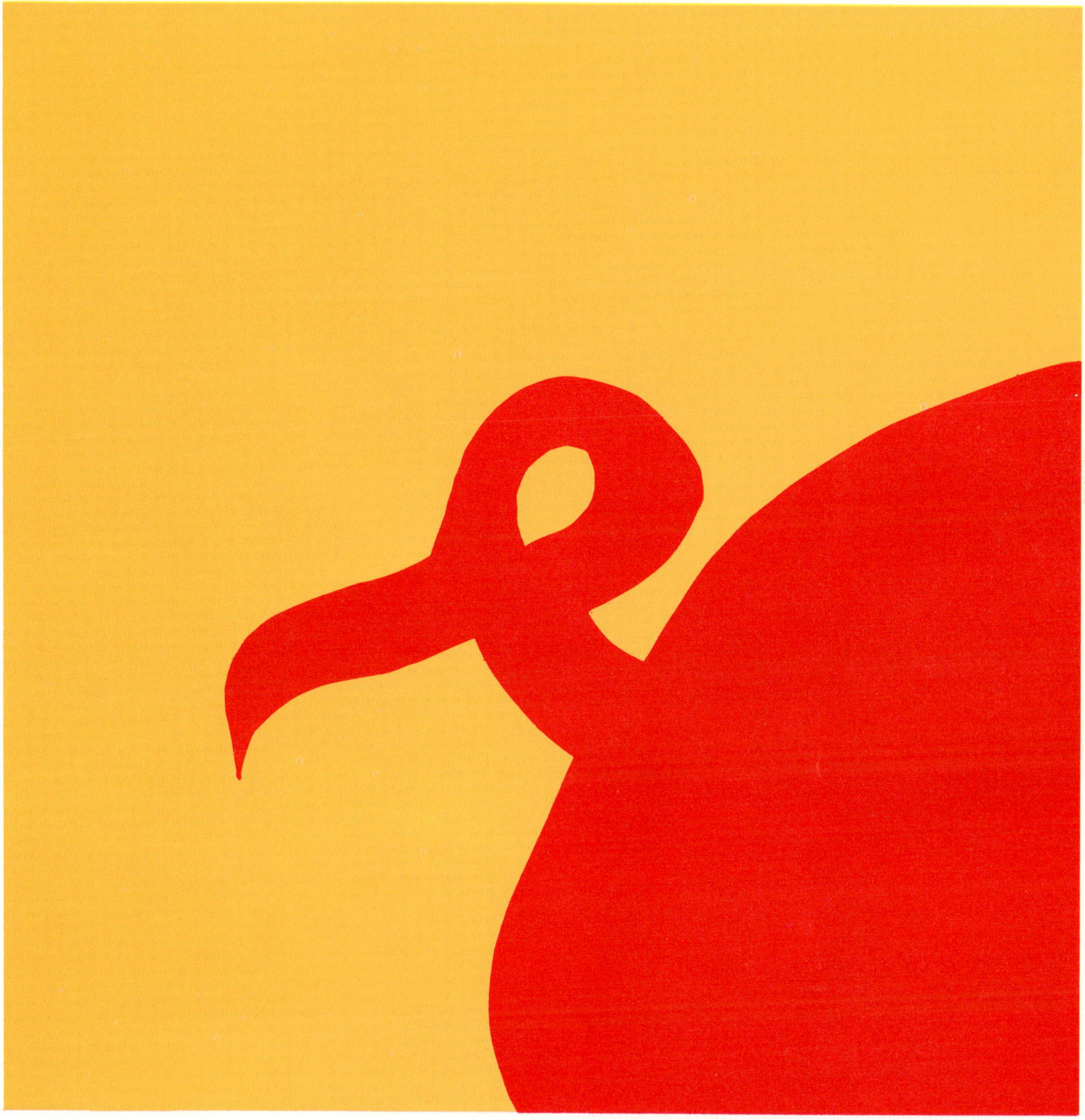

Pig

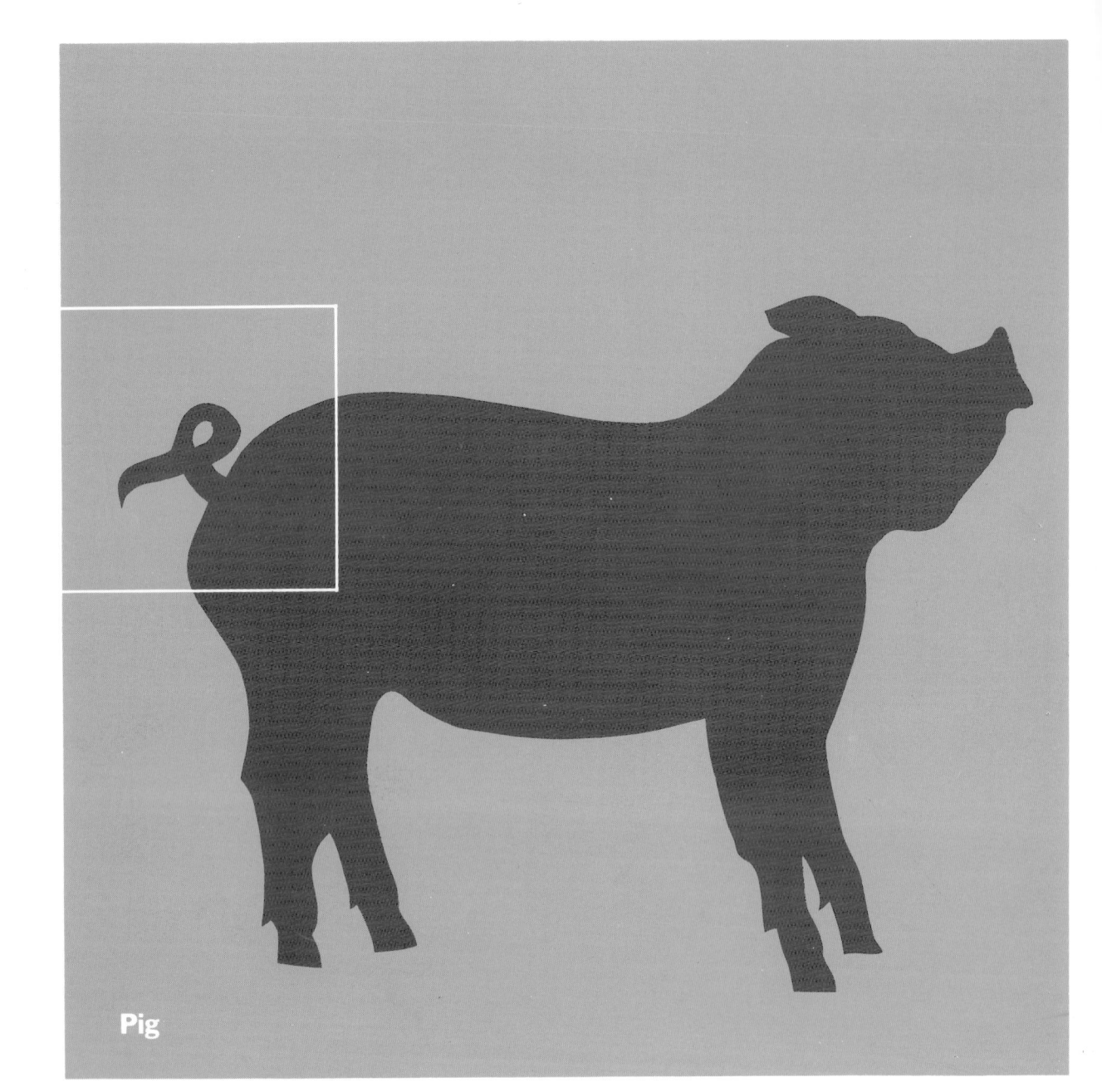

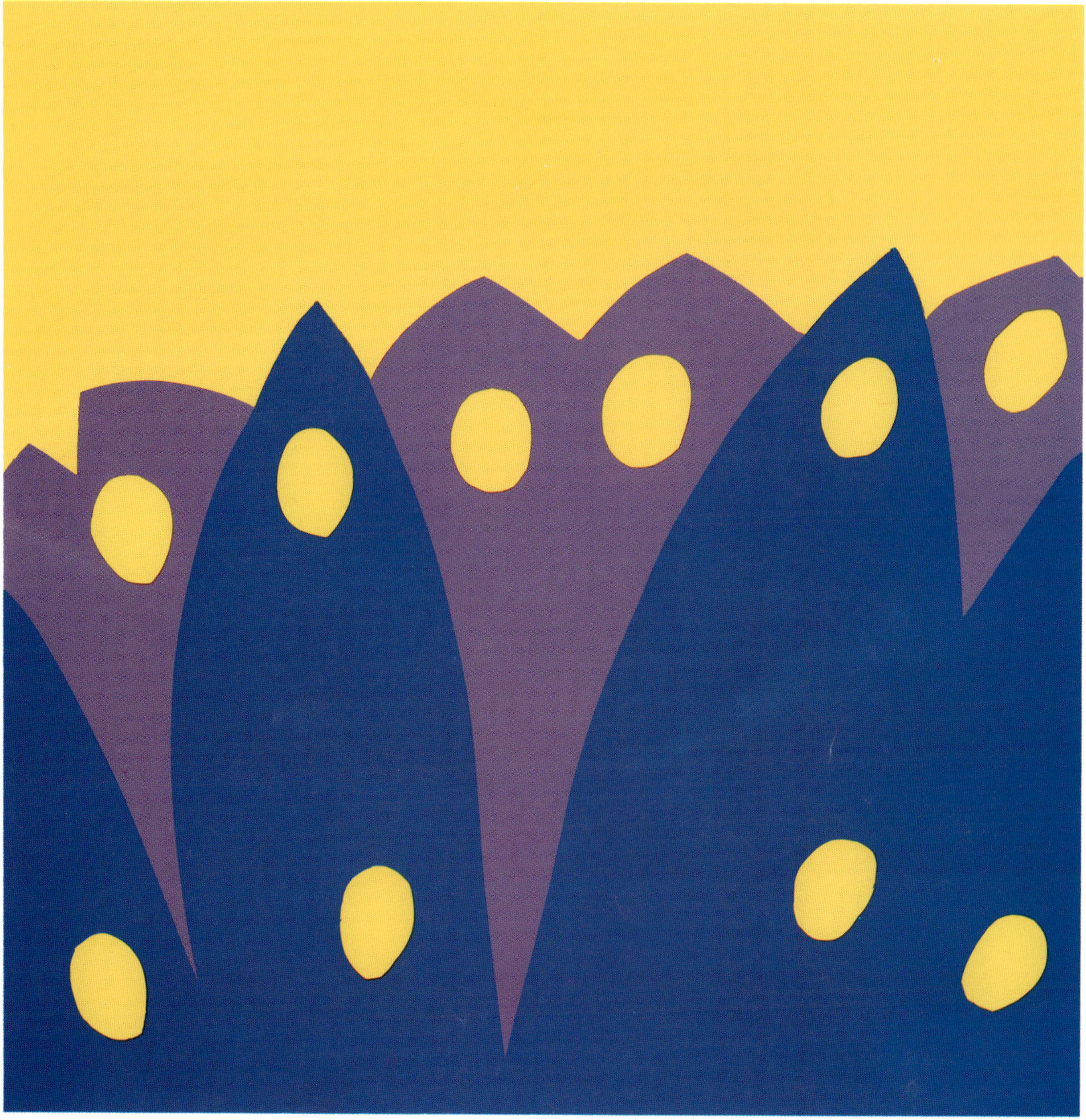

Peacock

About the Author

Beau Gardner was born in Oceanside, New York. He graduated from Pratt Institute, where he studied graphic design. In 1973 he started his own graphic design studio, Beau Gardner Associates, Inc., in New York City. His services to corporate clients have won him many major awards. He is the creator of three other books, *The Upside Down Riddle Book*, compiled by Louis Phillips, *The turn about, think about, look about book*, and *The look again…and again, and again, and again book*. *The Horn Book Magazine* has proclaimed Mr. Gardner's work "visual exercise in mind stretching," and *Newsweek* has said that he "plays lovely visual tricks." Mr. Gardner lives on Long Island with his wife and three daughters.